MEASURES *of* SUCCESS®

A Comprehensive Musicianship Band Method

DEBORAH A. SHELDON • BRIAN BALMAGES • TIMOTHY LOEST • ROBERT SHELDON
PERCUSSION WRITTEN AND EDITED BY DAVID COLLIER

Congratulations on completing the first book of *Measures of Success,* and welcome to Book 2! Throughout this book, you will explore music from many different countries around the world and learn about many composers that you did not encounter in Book 1. You will also explore some of the fascinating historical events and literature that help bring the days of these composers to life.

This book includes 2 accompaniment CDs that contain performance tracks with live musicians playing the music from your book, as well as accompaniment tracks so you can play along. Additional CDs that cover the remainder of the book can be purchased at your local music dealer or downloaded at www.fjhmusic.com/mos.

Enjoy this exciting time in your musical growth. As you practice, you will continue to find yourself sharing the gift of music with family, friends, and audiences.

Ready?

Let's make music!

Production: Frank J. Hackinson
Production Coordinators: Ken Mattis and Brian Balmages
Cover Design and Interior Line Drawings: Danielle Taylor and Adrianne Hirosky
Interior Layout and Design: Andi Whitmer
Engraving: Tempo Music Press, Inc.
Printer: Tempo Music Press, Inc.

ISBN-13: 978-1-56939-897-5

THE FJH MUSIC COMPANY INC.

Frank J. Hackinson

PRELUDE: THE WARM-UP

The **warm-up** prepares you for individual practice or rehearsal. Much as an athlete warms up before an event, musicians must do the same thing. Play these exercises with and without the CD each time you practice. Even as they become easier, focus on playing with a beautiful sound.

1. STEADY AS SHE GOES *Keep your tone steady and beautiful. Hold all notes for their full value.*

2. SOUND BUILDER *Use deep breathing to maintain a beautiful sound.*

3. HALF AND HALF

4. CHORALE – Trio or Full Band

5. CHORALE (BEFIEHL DU DEINE WEGE) – Full Band

J.S. Bach

✵ OPUS 1: RECAPITULATION

A **recapitulation** is a summary that restates the main points of a subject. In music, a recapitulation occurs after a development section and presents the main themes of a movement for a final time. Your musicianship developed substantially in Book 1, so the following recapitulation will reacquaint you with many of the concepts you have already learned.

LET'S REVIEW

The following music will help you to remember these important elements:

1.1 GIVE ME FIVE!

1.2 SUR LE PONT D'AVIGNON *Hold all notes for their full value.*

French Folk Song

1.3 THIS OLD MAN *Be sure to play complete phrases!*

English Folk Song

1.4 ORANGES AND LEMONS

English Folk Song

1.5 THEME FROM SONATA NO. 11

Wolfgang Amadeus Mozart

4

BB210BBC

LET'S REVIEW

The following music will help you to remember these important elements:

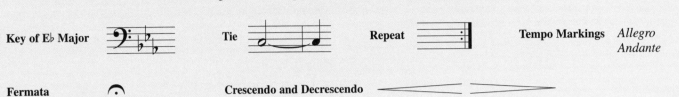

Key of E♭ Major   **Tie**   **Repeat**   **Tempo Markings** *Allegro*
Andante

Fermata   **Crescendo and Decrescendo**

1.6 FADING FANFARE

mp   *f*   *mf*   *p*

1.7 AURA LEE

American Folk Song

p   *mp*

mf

rit.

f   *p*

1.8 LOS POLLITOS

Mexican Folk Song

Allegro

f

HISTORY

MUSIC

Polish composer **Frédéric Chopin** (1810–1845), much like Mozart, was a musical prodigy who began composing at a very early age. He was an accomplished pianist and all of his works involve the piano. His *Fantaisie-Impromptu* is one of his best-known pieces, despite the fact he never wanted it to be published!

LITERATURE

In 1834, when *Fantaisie-Impromptu* was written, the great Russian poet and author Alexander Pushkin wrote the short story *The Queen of Spades,* a tale of human greed. Composers Tchaikovsky and Franz von Suppé both wrote operas based on Pushkin's story.

WORLD

In 1834, final modifications were made to the present form of Braille, a system used to help the blind read and write. Fish lovers sent up a cheer when sardines were canned for the first time in Europe.

1.9 FANTAISIE-IMPROMPTU

Frédéric Chopin

Andante

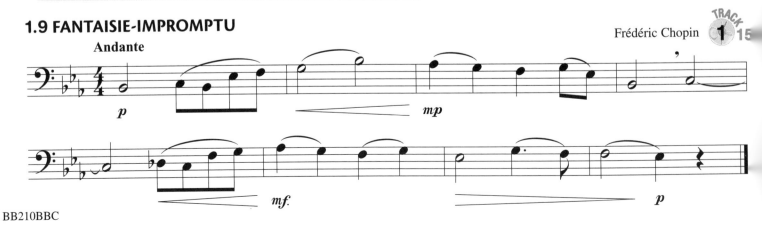

p   *mp*

mf   *p*

LET'S REVIEW
The following music will help you to remember these important elements:

Key of A♭ Major		Time Signature		Eighth Rest	↱
Tempo Marking	*Moderato*	Accent		Pick-up Note	

1.10 THEME FROM SYMPHONY NO. 1 – Duet

Moderato

Johannes Brahms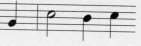

1.11 ALL NIGHT, ALL DAY

Andante

Traditional Spiritual

HISTORY

MUSIC
Jacques Offenbach (1819–1880) was born in Germany as "Jacob" but became "Jacques" when he moved to Paris to study cello at the Paris Conservatoire. He is best known for his operettas (he wrote almost 100 of them!), including *Orpheus in the Underworld,* which includes the famous *Can-can.*

LITERATURE
Henry Wadsworth Longfellow wrote the narrative poem *The Courtship of Miles Standish.* Standish was a passenger on the Mayflower and became Plymouth Colony's assistant governor. Just a few years later, Charles Dickens wrote *Great Expectations,* a story of an orphan boy named Pip who faced personal struggles that shaped his life and character.

WORLD
In 1858, a series of seven debates between Abraham Lincoln and Stephen Douglas were held in Illinois. That year, Minnesota was admitted to the union as the 32nd state. Pencils with attached erasers, as well as rotary washing machines, were patented.

1.12 CAN-CAN *Use your air to emphasize notes with accents.*

Allegro

Jacques Offenbach

1.13 CRIPPLE CREEK

Brightly

Appalachian Folk Song

1.14 THE MARINES' HYMN

March tempo

Official Song of the U.S. Marine Corps

BB210BBC

6

The following music will help you to remember these important elements:

1.15 THE MAN ON THE FLYING TRAPEZE *Play tenuto notes smoothly and connected.*   Gaston Lyle   TRACK 1 21

1.16 THE CUCKOO WOODPECKER *Play staccato notes lightly and separated.*   TRACK 1 22

1.17 BACKYARD STOMP   TRACK 1 23

1.18 TURKISH MARCH *Remember to change dynamics on the repeat.*   Wolfgang Amadeus Mozart   TRACK 1 24

1.19 FLOWER DRUM SONG   Chinese Folk Song   TRACK 1 25

1.20 TECHNIQUE TWISTER *Use good breath support and keep a steady beat. Try playing with a metronome!*   TRACK 1 26

LET'S REVIEW

The following music will help you to remember these important elements:

Chromatics and Accidentals

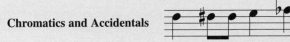

1.21 CHA-CHA CHROMATICA

TRACK 1 / 27

Allegro

1.22 TWO-FACED POLKA

TRACK 1 / 28

Moderato

Hey!

HISTORY

MUSIC

Hungarian Dance No. 5 comes from a set of 21 dances written by **Johannes Brahms** (1833–1897) and based mostly on Hungarian melodies. Ironically, Brahms accidentally based this piece on a folk dance by another composer, Kéler Béla, thinking that it was a traditional folk song.

LITERATURE

Leo Tolstoy wrote his epic novel *War and Peace,* a work of historical fiction that is considered a classic to this day. American novelist Louisa May Alcott, who is best known for writing *Little Women,* published the sequel entitled *Good Wives,* which followed the lives of the *Little Women* as they grew into adulthood.

WORLD

In 1869, the Suez Canal opened in Egypt. This man-made waterway connects the Mediterranean and Red Seas. John Willis Menard became the first African American to speak in Congress in that same year. The Cincinnati Red Stockings became the first professional baseball team in the United States.

1.23 HUNGARIAN DANCE NO. 5

Johannes Brahms

TRACK 1 / 29

Allegro

1.24 FINGER TWISTER

TRACK 1 / 30

OPUS 1 ENCORE!

INTERPRETATION STATION

Listen to CD 1 Track 31. You will hear two versions of each example.
Choose the version (A or B) that has better phrasing. Circle your answer.

1. A B   **2.** A B   **3.** A B   **4.** A B

SIMON "SEZ"

Listen to CD 1 Track 32. You will hear a well-known musical work. Listen first, sing it, then find the pitches on your instrument.
You can then play along with the accompaniment track that follows. Can you match the notes and style of the recording?

COMPOSER'S CORNER

Using only the notes from the Concert B♭ Major Scale, complete this composition. Refer to the time signature.
Remember to add dynamics. Give your piece a title and perform it for a friend or family member!

Title:_____   Name:_____

PENCIL POWER

In Opus 1, you reviewed many of the musical concepts you learned in *Measures of Success* Book 1.
Match each item on the left with its correct term or definition by writing in the appropriate letter.

1. _____ *Marziale*
2. _____
3. _____
4. _____ *Andante*
5. _____
6. _____ *Allegro*
7. _____ *rit.*
8. _____ $\frac{2}{4}$

9. _____
10. _____
11. _____
12. _____
13. _____
14. _____
15. _____
16. _____

A. Tenuto
B. Walking Tempo
C. Fast Tempo
D. Gradually Slow Down
E. Staccato
F. Gradually Get Louder
G. Fermata
H. Repeat

I. Pick-up Note
J. Slur
K. Accent
L. Eighth Rest
M. March Style
N. Breath Mark
O. Tie
P. Time Signature

CURTAIN UP!

Time to perform! Play this piece for friends or family members. Remember to introduce the piece by its title and bow when you are finished.

1.25 CHESTER

William Billings

OPUS 2

ARTICULATION REVISITED: STACCATO
Staccato eighth notes are played lightly and separated.

2.1 SEPARATION ANXIETY

2.2 THE GRUMPY PIRATE
Traditional Sea Shanty Melody

2.3 RUMBA CUBANA! *A rumba is a rhythmic Cuban dance that has Spanish and African origins.*

 ON THE PODIUM

CONDUCTING REVIEW: 4/4 TIME
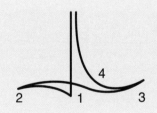

2.4 CHICKEN ON A FENCE POST
American Folk Song

 ON THE PODIUM

BB210BBC

HISTORY

MUSIC

George M. Cohan (1878–1942), known as "Mr. Broadway", wrote many musicals that were staged on Broadway in New York. His memorable melodies are still loved and sung today. Some of his most notable songs are *Yankee Doodle Dandy, Give My Regards to Broadway,* and *You're a Grand Old Flag,* a song that paid tribute to the U.S. flag and won him a Congressional Gold Medal in 1936.

LITERATURE

Eric Arthur Blair, who was better known by his pen name George Orwell, was a British author who made a profound impact on literature. Just after Cohan died, Orwell wrote *Animal Farm,* a story of corruption, greed and ignorance. It is considered to be among the greatest English-language novels ever written.

WORLD

In 1906, the world's first animated cartoon was released. In the same year, the first airplane flight in Europe took place in Paris, and the SOS international distress signal was adopted.

2.5 YOU'RE A GRAND OLD FLAG 🖉 *Circle the ♪♪♩♪ syncopations!* George M. Cohan TRACK 1 38

2.6 SUMMIT FANFARE TRACK 1 39

NEW NOTE! D

2.7 THE FOREST OWL Japanese Folk Song TRACK 1 40

2.8 LITTLE BROWN JUG Joseph E. Winner TRACK 1 4

RHYTHM

CUT TIME (ALLA BREVE)

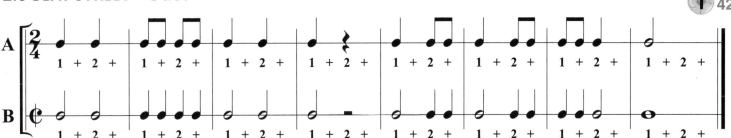

¢ = 2/2 = 2 beats in each measure.
Half note gets one beat.

2.9 BEAT STREET – Duet

TRACK 1 42

2.10 CUT IT OUT!

TRACK 1 43

HISTORY

MUSIC
Modest Mussorgsky (1839–1881), was a Russian composer whose music has a strong nationalistic flavor. The *Great Gate of Kiev* is the final movement of the larger work *Pictures at an Exhibition,* completed in 1874. It depicts a monumental gate designed for Tsar Alexander II.

LITERATURE
In 1874, French author Victor Hugo, who is famous for the novels *Les Misérables* and *The Hunchback of Notre Dame,* wrote *Ninety-Three,* a novel set in 1793 during the French Revolution. Around the same time, William Wells Brown wrote *The Rising Sun.* Brown is considered the first African-American to have published a novel.

WORLD
The first zoo in the U.S. opened in 1874 in Philadelphia, PA. Around the same time, P.T. Barnum's Circus (later to become the Barnum and Bailey Circus), the largest in the U.S., made its debut and began traveling the country by railroad.

2.11 THE GREAT GATE OF KIEV

Modest Mussorgsky TRACK 1 44

2.12 MANHATTAN BEACH

John Philip Sousa TRACK 1 45

CHORDS

A chord is comprised of three or more pitches played simultaneously. A **major chord** uses the 1ˢᵗ, 3ʳᵈ, and 5ᵗʰ notes of a major scale. A **minor chord** is created by lowering the 3ʳᵈ note of the scale one half step.

STYLE AND FORM: TRIO

A **trio** has three different parts performed simultaneously by three individuals or groups.

2.13 MOOD CHANGE – Trio *Listen to how the B line changes the tonality of the chords from major to minor.*

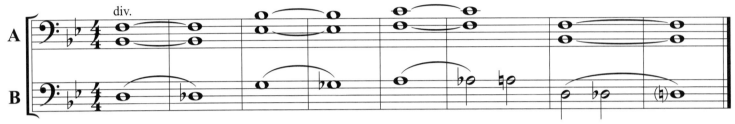

NATURAL AND HARMONIC MINOR SCALES

The **natural minor** scale has eight notes going up or down in consecutive order, all in the key signature of the scale name. In your key of G minor, all eight notes are in the key signature of G minor, which has 2 flats.
The **harmonic minor** scale raises the 7ᵗʰ scale note of a natural minor scale by one half step.

2.14 CONCERT G NATURAL MINOR SCALE, ARPEGGIO AND CHORD

2.15 CONCERT G HARMONIC MINOR SCALE, ARPEGGIO AND CHORD

2.16 MINKA

Russian Folk Song

2.17 THE DRONING BAGPIPES

 NEW NOTE! B

Andante

mf

NEW KEY SIGNATURE

This is the key of **C Major**.      This key signature indicates that there are no flats or sharps.

2.18 CONCERTO THEME

Ludwig van Beethoven

 Track 1 51

Legato

mp   *mf*   *mp*   *p*

2.19 CHEKI, MORENA

Puerto Rican Dance

Giocoso *(merry)*

f

CUT TIME SYNCOPATION

Remember that weak beats are stressed in syncopation. Look at these examples.
Keeping a steady beat, clap and count the rhythm for each. They sound the same!

1 + 2 +

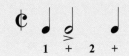

1 + 2 +

2.20 CHEKI, MORENA OTRA VEZ!

Puerto Rican Dance

 Track 1 53

Giocoso

f

14

HISTORY

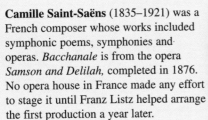

MUSIC

Camille Saint-Saëns (1835–1921) was a French composer whose works included symphonic poems, symphonies and operas. *Bacchanale* is from the opera *Samson and Delilah,* completed in 1876. No opera house in France made any effort to stage it until Franz Listz helped arrange the first production a year later.

LITERATURE

Anna Sewell's novel *Black Beauty* was published in 1877. It was Sewell's first and only novel. Since its publication, millions of readers have enjoyed this book, a horse's memoir. It has become one of the best-selling books in the world.

WORLD

In 1877, Thomas Edison invented the Edisonphone, a tin cylinder phonograph that made the first recording. Also in 1877, the oldest tennis tournament in the world, Wimbledon, held its first men's tennis match.

2.21 BACCHANALE FROM SAMSON AND DELILAH

Notice the counting in measure 11 for the dotted half note.

Camille Saint-Saëns

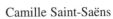

2.22 CHROMAT-ATTACK (FIGHT SONG) – Duet

THEORY

IMPROVISATION

Improvisation occurs when performers compose and play music on the spot, without rehearsal and without reading notation.

2.23 KLEZMER! – Improvisation

Use the guide notes to improvise while a partner plays the music below, or play along with the CD. (Note: The CD recording repeats 4 times.)

BB210BBC

OPUS 2 ENCORE!

INTERPRETATION STATION

Listen to CD 1 Track 57. You will hear pairs of chords or scales. Listen to each pair, comparing the second example to the first. Decide if the second example in each pair is Major or minor. Circle your answers.

1. Major minor   2. Major minor   3. Major minor   4. Major minor

SIMON "SEZ"

Listen to CD 1 Track 58. You will hear a well-known musical work. Listen first, sing it, then find the pitches on your instrument. You can then play along with the accompaniment track that follows. Can you match the notes and style of the recording?

COMPOSER'S CORNER

Using your knowledge of Major and minor, transform *London Bridge* into *Lonely Bridge* by rewriting it in a minor key. Think about which notes will need accidentals. The first two measures have already been completed for you!

LONDON BRIDGE

Traditional

LONELY BRIDGE

PENCIL POWER – CREATING MAJOR AND MINOR CHORDS

Decide if the chord is Major or minor. Circle your answer. Be careful! Example 5 is tricky!

1.  2.  3.  4.  5.

Major minor   Major minor   Major minor   Major minor   Major minor

Correctly add notes to create the chord. Be careful! Example 10 is tricky!

6.  7. 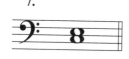 8.  9.  10.

E♭ Major   C Major   B♭ minor   A♭ Major   E♭ minor

SIGHT READING

Sight reading is a way to demonstrate what you know about reading and performing music. Remember the **Three Ps** to help you sight read:

Preview: Title, composer, key signature, time signature, tempo, style, articulation and expression markings
Process: Imagine the flow of the music, silently fingering through transitions and complex passages
Perform: Set your posture and embouchure, then play the passage as musically as possible

2.24 ELEMENTS – Sight Reading

CURTAIN UP! FULL BAND

2.25 MARCHE MILITAIRE

Franz Schubert
arr. Robert Sheldon

2.26 SUNSET ON THE CHESAPEAKE

Brian Balmages

OPUS 3

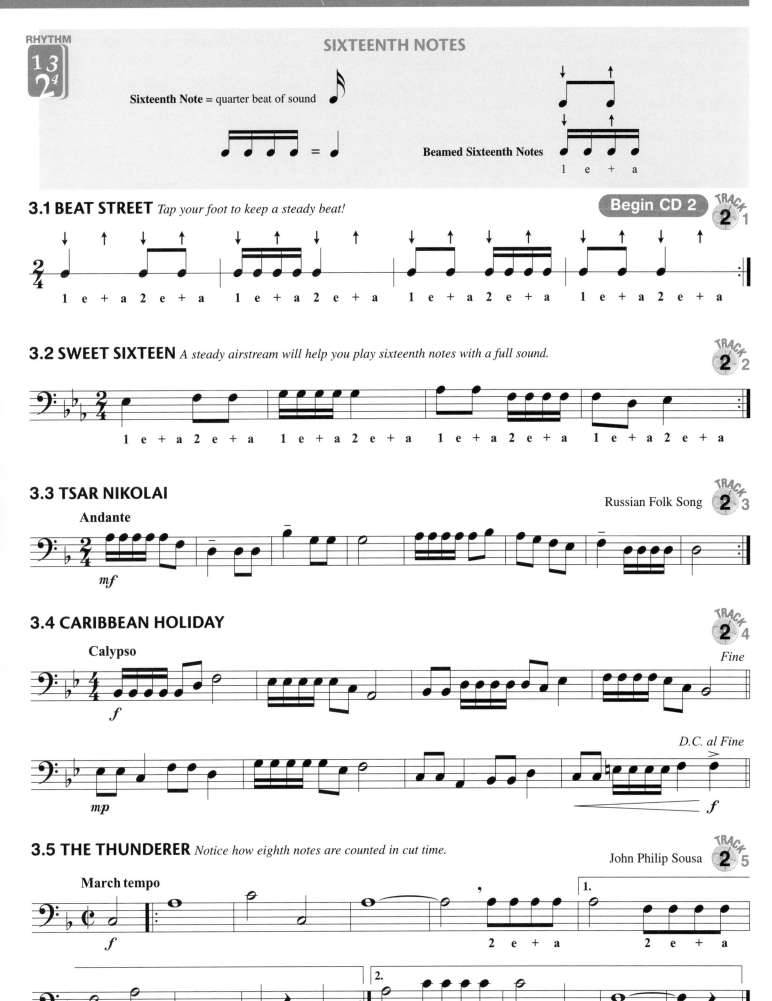

RHYTHM 13 2/4

SIXTEENTH NOTES

Sixteenth Note = quarter beat of sound

Beamed Sixteenth Notes

1 e + a

3.1 BEAT STREET *Tap your foot to keep a steady beat!*

Begin CD 2 — TRACK 2/1

1 e + a 2 e + a   1 e + a 2 e + a   1 e + a 2 e + a   1 e + a 2 e + a

3.2 SWEET SIXTEEN *A steady airstream will help you play sixteenth notes with a full sound.*

TRACK 2/2

1 e + a 2 e + a   1 e + a 2 e + a   1 e + a 2 e + a   1 e + a 2 e + a

3.3 TSAR NIKOLAI

Russian Folk Song — TRACK 2/3

Andante

mf

3.4 CARIBBEAN HOLIDAY

TRACK 2/4

Calypso

Fine

f

D.C. al Fine

mp   *f*

3.5 THE THUNDERER *Notice how eighth notes are counted in cut time.*

John Philip Sousa — TRACK 2/5

March tempo

f   1.

2 e + a   2 e + a

2.

2 e + a

BB210BBC

EIGHTH NOTE/TWO SIXTEENTH NOTE GROUP

An eighth note can replace the first two sixteenth notes in a group of four sixteenth notes.
This creates an **eighth note/two sixteenth note group.**

3.6 BEAT STREET

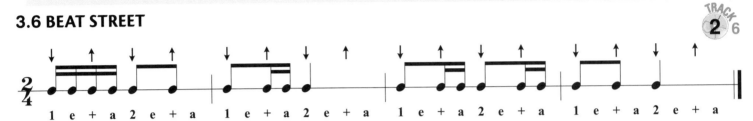

3.7 16TH STREET *Remember to use a steady airstream.*

ONE-MEASURE REPEAT

% Repeat the preceding measure.

3.8 THE KING'S TRUPETERS – Duet

CONDUCTING REVIEW: ¾ TIME

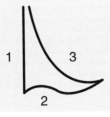

3.9 THE MATADOR

HISTORY

MUSIC

Trepak, based on a Ukrainian folk dance, is part of the famous ballet *The Nutcracker,* written by **Pyotr I. Tchaikovsky** (1840–1893). Based on Hoffman's *The Nutcracker and the Mouse King,* it remains a favorite among listeners, especially during the holidays.

LITERATURE

Scottish author Robert Louis Stevenson introduced the world to the fictitious pirate, Long John Silver, in his novel *Treasure Island.* This adventure tells the tale of pirates and buried gold. Also, J.R.R. Tolkien, author of *The Hobbit* and *Lord of the Rings,* was born the same year *The Nutcracker* was premiered.

WORLD

In 1892, Ellis Island became the official welcome center for immigrants to the U.S., Fig Newtons® were first produced and to make sure you had a sparkling smile after you ate them, the toothpaste tube was invented!

3.10 TREPAK

Pytor I. Tchaikovsky — TRACK **2** 10

3.11 OLD JOE CLARK

American Folk Song — TRACK **2** 11

NEW NOTE! Db

HISTORY

MUSIC

Green Bushes is an English folk song that has been used by several composers. **Percy Grainger** (1882–1961) was a composer born in Australia who wrote some of the most notable works in the wind band literature. He used *Green Bushes* in several of his works including *Lincolnshire Posy* and *Green Bushes (Passacaglia on an English Folksong).*

LITERATURE

The children's novel *A Little Princess* was written by Frances Hodgson Burnett. American author Jack London wrote his most famous novel, *The Call of the Wild,* a story about a domesticated dog that eventually turns back into a wild animal. London soon followed with a companion novel, *White Fang.*

WORLD

Around the turn of the century, the Canadian provinces of Saskatchewan and Alberta were established. Front-wheel drive for automobiles was patented by a German engineer, and Las Vegas officially became a city in the U.S.

3.12 GREEN BUSHES

English Folk Song — TRACK **2** 12

20

TWO SIXTEENTH NOTE/EIGHTH NOTE GROUP

An eighth note can replace the last two sixteenth notes in a group of four sixteenth notes. This creates a **two sixteenth note/eighth note group**.

3.13 BEAT STREET

3.14 ANOTHER WAY *Remember to use a steady airstream.*

3.15 STODOLA PUMPA
Czech Folk Song

3.16 LA MORISQUE
Tielman Susato

3.17 SKYWARD

3.18 THE MOREEN
Irish Air

CONDUCTING REVIEW: 2/4 TIME

3.19 JIM ALONG JOSEY
American Folk Song

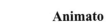

BB210BBC

3.20 SQUARE DANCE – Duet

KEY CHANGE

A **key change** occurs when music moves from one key to another in a single musical work. You will know a key change has occurred when you see a double bar line followed by a new key signature. The new key signature shows the new sharps or flats and may also contain natural signs that cancel the sharps or flats from the previous key signature.

3.21 CHANGE UP (CONCERT F TO B♭ MAJOR)

key change

3.22 DECK THE HALLS *What is the starting key signature? What is the ending key signature?*

Welsh Carol

BB210BBC

3.23 CHILDREN'S PRAYER FROM HANSEL AND GRETEL

Engelbert Humperdinck

TRACK 2 23

3.24 PATAPAN

Bernard de la Monnoye

TRACK 2 24

3.25 LONG ROAD HOME
Diminuendo – abbreviated "*dim.*" – means to gradually play softer, similar to decrescendo (*decresc.*).

TRACK 2 25

3.26 CHROMATIC SCHEMATIC

TRACK 2 26

3.27 ROCK IT MY WAY – Improvisation

Use the guide notes provided to improvise your own melody. Have a friend play the accompaniment part or play along with the accompaniment track on the CD. Have fun! (Note: The CD recording repeats 2 times.)

guide notes

TRACK 2 27

open repeat

OPUS 3 ENCORE!

INTERPRETATION STATION

Listen to CD 2 Track 28. You will hear a tempo given by a click track. This is the speed of the quarter note. After each click track you will hear a rhythm. Select which notated rhythm is being played and write the corresponding answer letter on the line. Each example is performed twice.

1. _____   3. _____

2. _____   4. _____

SIMON "SEZ"

Listen to CD 2 Track 29. You will hear a well-known musical work. Listen first, sing it, then find the pitches on your instrument. You can then play along with the accompaniment track that follows. Can you match the notes and style of the recording?

COMPOSER'S CORNER

Many composers use key changes as a compositional technique. Rewrite this melody in the key of Concert E♭ Major. Then play the entire piece!

SWEETLY SINGS THE DONKEY

Traditional

PENCIL POWER

Rewrite the following musical examples in either 2/4 or cut time. Pay attention to how you beam eighth notes and sixteenth notes!

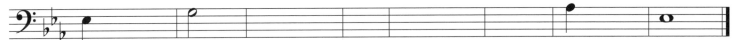

SIGHT READING

Remember the Three Ps to help you sight read: **Preview, Process, Perform.**

3.28 LINE OF SIGHT – Sight Reading

Moderato

CURTAIN UP!

3.29 BARN DANCE

Brian Balmages

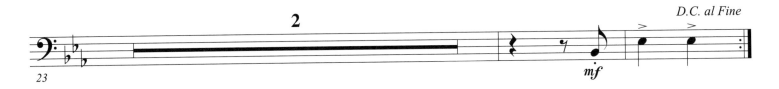

3.30 CLOUDS

Robert Sheldon

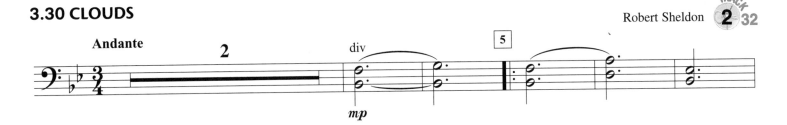

BB210BBC

✺ OPUS 4

MORE TIME SIGNATURES

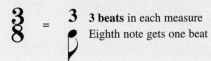

$\frac{3}{8}$ = **3** **3 beats** in each measure

Eighth note gets one beat

4.1 BEAT STREET – Duet

TRACK 2 33

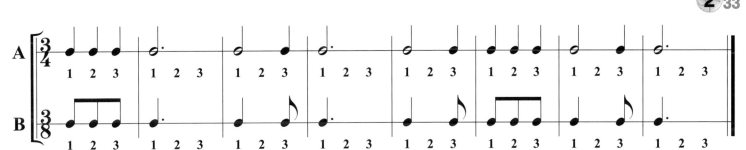

4.2 TRIPLE THREAT

TRACK 2 34

4.3 POP! GOES THE WEASEL

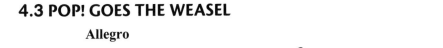

English Traditional TRACK 2 35

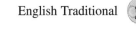

Allegro

mf

4.4 BRING A TORCH, JEANNETTE, ISABELLA

French Carol TRACK 2 36

ON THE PODIUM

Allegretto *(slightly slower than **Allegro**)*

mp

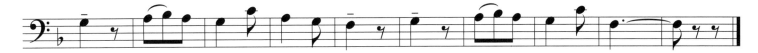

26

4.5 PARADE OF THE WOODEN SOLDIERS – Duet

Leon Jessel

4.6 WACKY WALTZ

RALLENTANDO

Rallentando – abbreviated "*rall.*" – means to gradually slow down, similar to ritardando (*rit.*).

4.7 DARK OVERTURE

4.8 TAFTA HINDI

Arabic Folk Song

4.9 À LA BAROQUE

BB210BBC

4.10 THE RAKES OF MALLOW

Irish Folk Song

D.C. AL CODA

Remember that D.C. is an abbreviation for *da capo*, an Italian term that refers to the beginning. A **coda** contains music that occurs at the end of a piece. **D.C. al Coda** means to return to the beginning and play until you come to the **coda sign,** ⊕. When you see the coda sign, skip to ⊕ **Coda** and play to the end.

4.11 GIVE MY REGARDS TO BROADWAY *Be sure to observe all the signs!*

George M. Cohan

4.12 IN A FUNK *Funk has roots in rhythm and blues. It was developed in the 1960s and 1970s and features strong bass lines.*

4.13 ROUGH WATERS

Andantino *(slightly faster than **Andante**)*

MORE TIME SIGNATURES

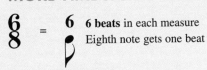

$\frac{6}{8}$ = **6** **6 beats** in each measure

♪ Eighth note gets one beat

In a faster tempo, emphasis is often placed on the 1st and 4th beats of each measure.
This gives the music a strong 2-beat pulse.

4.14 BEAT STREET

TRACK 2/46

4.15 ROYAL FANFARE

TRACK 2/47

Maestoso

4.16 LOOBY LOO *Conduct using a 2-beat pattern.*

Traditional   TRACK 2/48

ON THE PODIUM

Moderato

4.17 UN CANADIEN ERRANT

French-Canadian Folk Song   TRACK 2/49

Andantino

4.18 THE KERRY DANCE

Irish Folk Song   TRACK 2/50

Moderato

4.19 WALLABY STEW

Australian Folk Song

Allegretto

4.20 GRADUAL ASCENT

HISTORY

MUSIC
Bedřich Smetana (1824–1884) was a musical hero to the Czech people. He wrote music with a very strong nationalistic flavor. *The Moldau,* premiered in 1875, is a movement of his larger work *Má vlast (My Motherland).* It represents the beauty and strength of the great Bohemian Moldau river.

LITERATURE
American poet and master of the macabre Edgar Allan Poe, who died in 1849, was exhumed and reburied in 1875 in order to dedicate a grave marker to him. Almost fittingly, controversy still exists on whether or not the right body was reburied.

WORLD
In 1875, the English Channel was conquered by swimmer Matthew Webb. Folks with tummy troubles had new relief as Phillips'® Milk of Magnesia was introduced (it is still available in drug stores today!).

4.21 THEME FROM THE MOLDAU – Duet

Bedřich Smetana

Andante

BB210BBC

30

DOTTED EIGHTH NOTE/SIXTEENTH NOTE GROUP

Adding a dot after a note increases the length of the note by half of its value.
Here the dot is used with an eighth note to create a **dotted eighth note.**

4.22 BEAT STREET – Duet

TRACK **2** 54

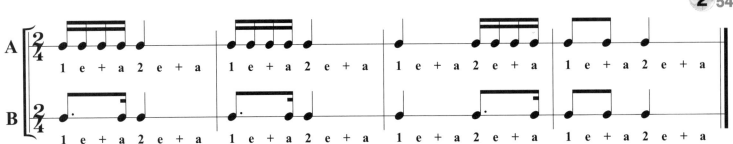

4.23 REGIMENT – Duet

TRACK **2** 55

4.24 COUNTRY GARDENS

English Folk Song   TRACK **2** 56

A TEMPO

The term **a tempo** means to return to the previous tempo.

4.25 LA DONNA È MOBILE

Giuseppe Verdi   TRACK **2** 57

BB210BBC

HISTORY

MUSIC

Richard Wagner (1813–1883) was a German composer who wrote music noted for its rich harmonies and thick textures. Wagner's opera *Lohengrin*, first performed in 1850, contains the well-known *Wedding March* which is still a popular processional at many weddings.

LITERATURE

Poet Alfred Lord Tennyson became the United Kingdom's Poet Laureate in 1850. A high honor, the Poet Laureate is an official appointment bestowed by the government on a poet of great stature, who is called upon to write poems that commemorate important national events. In the U.S., American abolitionist and author Harriet Beecher Stowe wrote *Uncle Tom's Cabin*, sparking a national debate on slavery.

WORLD

In 1850, Australia's oldest university, the University of Sydney, was founded. At the same time, Harriet Tubman was deemed the official conductor of the Underground Railroad.

4.26 BRIDAL CHORUS FROM LOHENGRIN

Richard Wagner

HISTORY

MUSIC

Franz Schubert (1797–1828) had only completed two movements of his *Symphony No. 8* ("*Unfinished*") before he left it for good. Other composers have offered versions of the complete symphony. No one really knows why Schubert did not finish the work. It is a musical mystery!

LITERATURE

Scottish author Sir Walter Scott wrote *Ivanhoe,* a novel in which Robin Hood made his first appearance. The story helped shape the modern concept of him as a cheerful, noble outlaw. At the same time, Catharine Sedgwick was writing novels and short stories in the United States. She was a champion of Republican motherhood, believing that mothers had a civic duty to raise children to be model citizens.

WORLD

In 1822, the United States officially recognized Mexico as an autonomous country. Dinosaur fossils and skeletons were discovered on the east coast of the U.S.

4.27 THEME FROM SYMPHONY NO. 8

Franz Schubert

4.28 TARANTELLA

Italian Folk Song

4.29 CHANT – Improvisation

Use the guide notes to improvise while a partner plays the music below, or play along with the CD. (Note: The CD recording repeats 4 times.)

BB210BBC

OPUS 4 ENCORE!

INTERPRETATION STATION

Listen to CD 2 Track 62. For each example, determine the time signature. Circle your answer.

1. $\frac{2}{4}$ $\frac{3}{8}$ 2. $\frac{6}{8}$ $\frac{4}{4}$ 3. $\frac{3}{4}$ ¢   4. ¢ $\frac{3}{8}$

SIMON "SEZ"

Listen to CD 2 Track 63. You will hear a well-known musical work. Listen first, sing it, then find the pitches on your instrument. You can then play along with the accompaniment track that follows. Can you match the notes and style of the recording?

COMPOSER'S CORNER

Write a melody for this duet using the guide notes provided. Pair up with a friend and perform it for your class or family!

Choose from these guide notes:

Title: _____   Composer: _____

PENCIL POWER

Match each definition with its correct term or symbol by writing in the appropriate letter.

1. _____ Two beats in each measure; half note gets one beat
2. _____ Three or more pitches sounding simultaneously
3. _____ Three different parts performed simultaneously by three different individuals or groups
4. _____ Merry
5. _____ Playing music on the spot without rehearsal or notation
6. _____ Three beats in each measure; eighth note gets one beat
7. _____ Slightly slower than *Allegro*
8. _____ Coda
9. _____ Faster than *Allegro*
10. _____ Animated or lively

A. Animato

B. Presto

C. ⊕

D. Giocoso

E. $\frac{3}{8}$

F. Trio

G. Allegretto

H. ¢

I. Chord

J. Improvisation

SIGHT READING

Remember the Three Ps to help you sight read: **Preview, Process, Perform.**

4.30 DANZA – Sight Reading

CURTAIN UP! FULL BAND

4.31 GARRYOWEN *The jig, a popular dance originating in Ireland and Scotland, has a variety of repeated motions and is often set in 6/8 time.*

Irish Folk Song
arr. Robert Sheldon

TRACK 2 65

4.32 AMERICA, THE BEAUTIFUL *Molto is an Italian term that means "very much."*

Samuel A. Ward
arr. Brian Balmages

TRACK 2 66

BB210BBC

5.1 TOP OF THE MORNING

NEW NOTE! E

Moderato

E

mf

5.2 ENTER THE NOBLES

Maestoso

mf ◁ f   mf ◁ f

RHYTHM 13 2 4

DOTTED QUARTER NOTE/EIGHTH NOTE GROUP IN CUT TIME

Keeping a steady beat, clap and count the rhythm for each example. They sound the same!

1 (e +) a   2 (e +) a   1 (e +) a   2 (e +) a

5.3 NOBLE PROCESSIONAL *Compare this piece to line 5.2. Do they sound the same?*

Maestoso

mf ◁ f   mf ◁ f

5.4 AIKEN DRUM

Scottish Folk Song

Allegretto

mf

5.5 BLOW THE MAN DOWN

Sea Shanty

ON THE PODIUM

Moderato

mf

BB210BBC

HISTORY

MUSIC	LITERATURE	WORLD
Antonio Vivaldi (1678–1741) was a composer of the Baroque style. He was a highly skilled violinist and spent most of his life in Venice, Italy. *Autumn* is from a set of violin concertos entitled *The Four Seasons*. It was published in 1725. Vivaldi wrote each movement to be reminiscent of each season of the year. 	Jonathan Swift was an Irish writer who was known as a master of satire. His novel *Gulliver's Travels* became incredibly popular as soon as it was published and continues to be one of his best-known works.	In 1723, Maryland required the establishment of public schools in all counties. A few years later across the Atlantic Ocean, France suffered from a famine and workers rioted when the price of bread was raised substantially. The coffeehouse craze was in full force in London, which had almost 2,000 of them!

5.12 AUTUMN FROM THE FOUR SEASONS

Antonio Vivaldi

THEORY

D.S. AL CODA

D.S. is an abbreviation for the Italian term *dal segno* or the sign, 𝄋. **D.S. al Coda** means to return to the sign (𝄋) and play until you come to the coda sign, 𝄌. When you see the coda sign, skip to the coda and play to the end.

5.13 DOWN BY THE STATION *Be sure to observe all the signs!*

American Folk Song

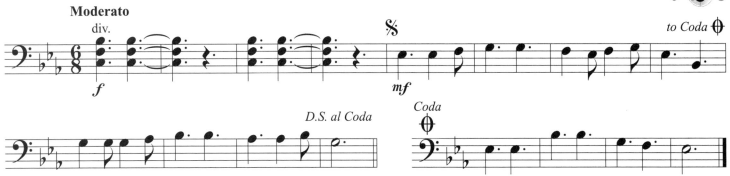

HISTORY

MUSIC	LITERATURE	WORLD
Johann Strauss I (1804–1849) was an Austrian composer whose legacy included many waltzes and the famous *Radetzky March,* which became quite popular among soldiers at the time. When Austrian officers first heard it, they clapped along with the chorus. This tradition is still carried on today. 	Alexandre Dumas, one of France's most renowned writers, wrote *The Queen's Necklace* in 1848. Dumas' most recognizable tales are *The Count of Monte Cristo* and *The Three Musketeers,* the latter telling of a young man named d'Artagnan who leaves home to become a guard of the musketeers.	In 1848, the saxophone was patented, Spain opened its first railroad, and the first Women's Rights convention was held in New York.

5.14 RADETZKY MARCH

Johann Strauss I

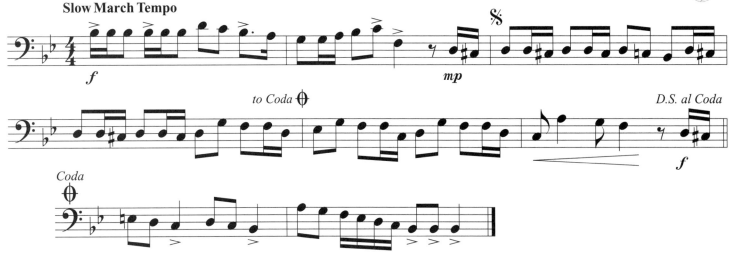

5.20 AN AUSTRIAN WENT YODELING

Austrian Folk Song

5.21 MARYBOROUGH MINER

Australian Folk Song

5.22 SHABBAT SHALOM

Israeli Folk Song

5.23 BATTLE HYMN OF THE REPUBLIC

Traditional American Melody

5.24 BLUES ROCK – Improvisation

The guide notes provided form a blues scale. Play the notes moving up and down a few times. Then use the notes to improvise your own melody. Have a friend play the accompaniment part or play along with the accompaniment track on the CD. Have fun! (Note: The CD recording repeats 3 times.)

OPUS 5 ENCORE!

INTERPRETATION STATION

Listen to CD 3 Track 20. Each example uses one of the musical elements below. Write the corresponding letter in the space provided.

1. _____ 2. _____ 3. _____ 4. _____

A. Diminuendo **B.** Molto ritardando **C.** Eighth note triplets **D.** Sixteenth notes

SIMON "SEZ"

Listen to CD 3 Track 21. You will hear a well-known musical work. Listen first, sing it, then find the pitches on your instrument. You can then play along with the accompaniment track that follows. Can you match the notes and style of the recording?

COMPOSER'S CORNER

A fanfare is a short musical flourish usually used for processions or grand entrances. Write a fanfare for your instrument in the key of Concert A♭ Major. Use at least two sets of eighth note triplets in your music. Title your piece and perform it for family and friends. *Hint: Don't forget the D.S. al Coda!*

Title: _____ Composer: _____

PENCIL POWER

Study each example and decide its time signature. Write the time signature in the appropriate place on the staff.

1.

3.

2. *Two time signatures will work for this example. Use both.*

4. *Bonus: This example uses a time signature that you have never seen. Can you figure it out?*

SIGHT READING

Remember the Three Ps to help you sight read: **Preview, Process, Perform.**

5.25 INTRADA – Sight Reading

BB210BBC

CURTAIN UP!

Ludwig van Beethoven
arr. Brian Balmages

5.27 CIRCUS DAZE

Robert Sheldon

OPUS 6

METER CHANGES

You have already played pieces with variations that use a meter change.
Sometimes the meter can change within the main melody. Remember these hints:

- Look ahead as you play.
- Check the bottom number of each time signature to determine what kind of note gets one beat.
- Watch your conductor!

6.1 PROMENADE FROM PICTURES AT AN EXHIBITION *Bonus: Conduct this piece!*

Modest Mussorgsky TRACK 3 25

6.2 FUM, FUM, FUM

Spanish Carol TRACK 3 26

6.3 SHENANDOAH

American Folk Song TRACK 3 27

6.4 SLITHERY SNAKE

TRACK 3 28

6.5 NIGHT ON BALD MOUNTAIN

Modest Mussorgsky TRACK 3 29

6.6 MARCH OF THE TOREADORS

Georges Bizet

Moderato

6.7 O TANNENBAUM

German Folk Song

Andante

6.8 MOUNTAIN CLIMBING

NEW NOTE! F

6.9 THE BRITISH GRENADIERS

English Marching Song

Stately

HISTORY

MUSIC

English composer **Sir Edward Elgar** (1857–1934) was one of the first composers to take advantage of new technology by recording many of his works to phonograph discs in the early 1900s. His famous march *Pomp and Circumstance* was premiered in 1901 and is often heard at graduation ceremonies.

LITERATURE

In 1901, American naturalist John Muir published *Our National Parks,* a collection of essays that helped conservation advocacy. *The Tale of Peter Rabbit* was privately published by Beatrix Potter. It was so successful that a publishing company accepted it a year later.

WORLD

British engineer Hubert Booth invented and patented a horse-drawn, house-to-house vacuum cleaner. William S. Harley created a drawing of an engine designed to fit a bicycle. This would be the prototype of the first Harley motorcycle.

6.10 POMP AND CIRCUMSTANCE

Sir Edward Elgar

Stately

6.11 MARCH FROM THE NUTCRACKER

Pytor I. Tchaikovsky

Moderato

6.12 WHEN JOHNNY COMES MARCHING HOME

American Folk Song

Victoriously

HISTORY

MUSIC

Blow Away the Morning Dew (also known as *The Baffled Knight*) is an English folk song dating back to the early 1600s. British composer **Ralph Vaughan Williams** (1872–1958) used it as one of the main melodies in the third movement of *English Folk Song Suite,* which he wrote for military band in 1923.

LITERATURE

In 1911, English playwright and author Frances Hodgson Burnett published *The Secret Garden,* which has become a classic of children's literature. In 1923, Austrian author Felix Salten wrote the novel *Bambi, A Life in the Woods.* This went on to become a successful Disney animated feature.

WORLD

Time magazine was first published in 1923. It was a big year for candy lovers. Reese's® Peanut Butter Cups, Butterfinger®, and Milky Way® bars were all invented!

6.13 BLOW AWAY THE MORNING DEW

English Folk Song

Allegretto

BB210BBC

HISTORY

MUSIC	LITERATURE	WORLD
Nikolai Rimsky-Korsakov (1844–1908) was a Russian composer who was also a master of orchestration. *Procession of the Nobles* is from the opera *Mlada*, which had a score that was divided between several composers. The entire project was never completed, yet this remains a popular work.	American author Stephen Crane wrote the war novel *The Red Badge of Courage* in 1895. The story illustrates the harshness of the American Civil War and has become one of the most influential works in American literature. Ironically, Crane was not born until after the war ended.	In 1895, Caroline Willard Baldwin became the first woman to earn a doctor of science degree at Cornell University. Around the same time, William Wrigley Jr. introduced Juicy Fruit® and Wrigley's Spearmint® chewing gum.

6.14 PROCESSION OF THE NOBLES

Nikolai Rimsky-Korsakov

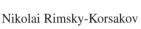

Pomposo *(grand and dignified)*

6.15 THE STAR-SPANGLED BANNER

U.S. National Anthem

Stately

6.16 "FINISHED THE BOOK" BLUES – Improvisation

As in Opus 5, the guide notes provided form a blues scale.
The accompaniment part is an example of a "walking bass line,"
which is common in swing. Have a friend play the accompaniment part,
or play along with the accompaniment track on the CD. Have fun! (Note: The CD recording repeats 2 times.)

guide notes

Swing

OPUS 6 ENCORE!

INTERPRETATION STATION

TRACK 3 41

Listen to CD 3 Track 41. For each example, decide which term best fits the music. Circle your answer.

1. Espressivo
   Maestoso

2. Pesante
   Andantino

3. Marziale
   Legato

4. Giocoso
   Cantabile

SIMON "SEZ"

TRACK 3 42

Listen to CD 3 Track 42. You will hear a well-known musical work. Listen first, sing it, and then find the pitches on your instrument. You can then play along with the accompaniment track that follows. Can you match the notes and style of the recording?

COMPOSER'S CORNER

Write a melody in the key of Concert G minor. Make sure that you have the correct number of beats in each measure by paying attention to the meter changes. Don't forget to add dynamics and articulations. Title your piece and perform it for family and friends.

Title: _____   Composer: _____

PENCIL POWER – MATCH THE COMPOSER

Match each composition with its composer by writing in the appropriate letter. Be careful! There are more composers than there are compositions!

1. _____ Trepak
2. _____ Bacchanale from Samson and Delilah
3. _____ La Donna è Mobile
4. _____ Pomp and Circumstance
5. _____ Hungarian Dance No. 5
6. _____ Procession of the Nobles
7. _____ The Great Gate of Kiev
8. _____ The Moldau
9. _____ Bridal Chorus from Lohengrin
10. _____ Give My Regards to Broadway

A. Elgar
B. Mussorgsky
C. Wagner
D. Smetana
E. Saint-Saëns
F. Offenbach

G. Cohan
H. Rimsky-Korsakov
I. Tchaikovsky
J. Brahms
K. Verdi
L. Strauss

SIGHT READING

Remember the Three P's to help you sight read: **Preview, Process, Perform**

6.17 CHANGES – Sight Reading

TRACK 3 43

CURTAIN UP!

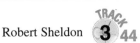

6.18 ZIMBABWE!

Robert Sheldon

TRACK 3 / 44

Rhythmic African Groove

6.19 FIREBOLT FANFARE

Brian Balmages

BB210BBC

6.20 MINUET AND TRIO FROM MUSIC FOR THE ROYAL FIREWORKS

Instrumental Solo

George Frideric Handel
arr. Brian Balmages

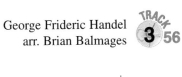

(no repeats on D.C.)

Fine

D.C. al Fine

6.20 MINUET AND TRIO FROM MUSIC FOR THE ROYAL FIREWORKS

Piano Accompaniment

George Frideric Handel
arr. Brian Balmages

SCALES AND ARPEGGIOS

CONCERT B♭ MAJOR AND RELATIVE MINOR

CONCERT B♭ MAJOR

CONCERT G NATURAL MINOR

CONCERT G HARMONIC MINOR

CONCERT G MELODIC MINOR

CONCERT E♭ MAJOR AND RELATIVE MINOR

CONCERT E♭ MAJOR

CONCERT C NATURAL MINOR

CONCERT C HARMONIC MINOR

CONCERT C MELODIC MINOR

CONCERT A♭ MAJOR AND RELATIVE MINOR

CONCERT A♭ MAJOR

CONCERT F NATURAL MINOR

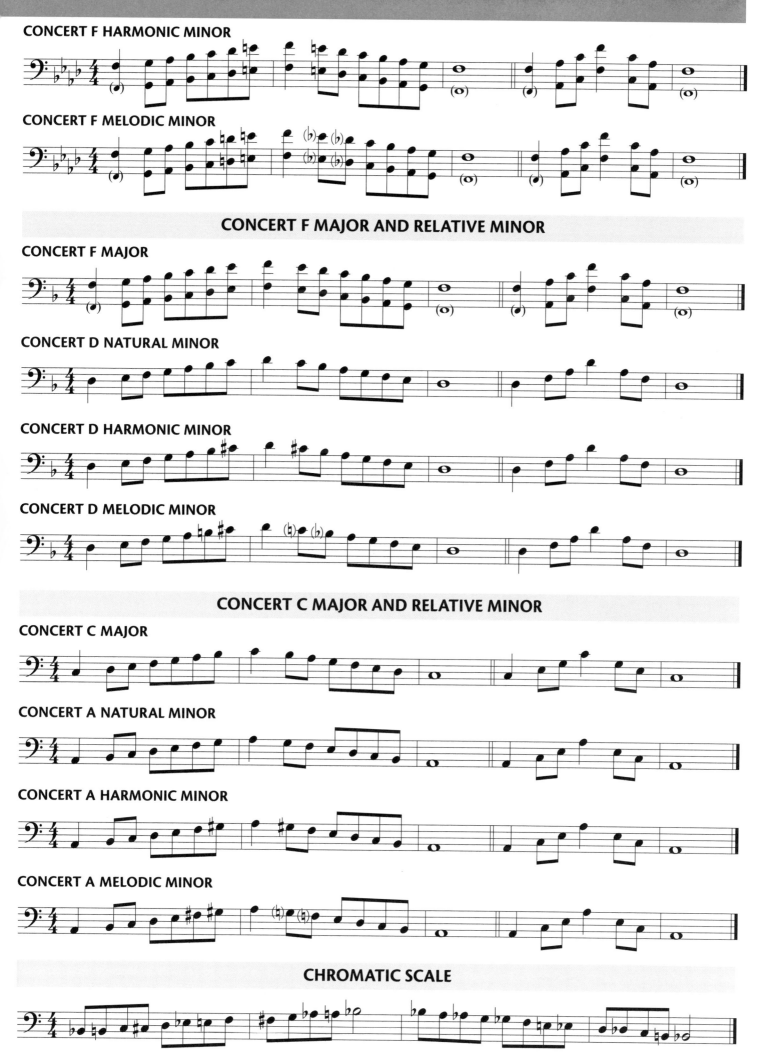

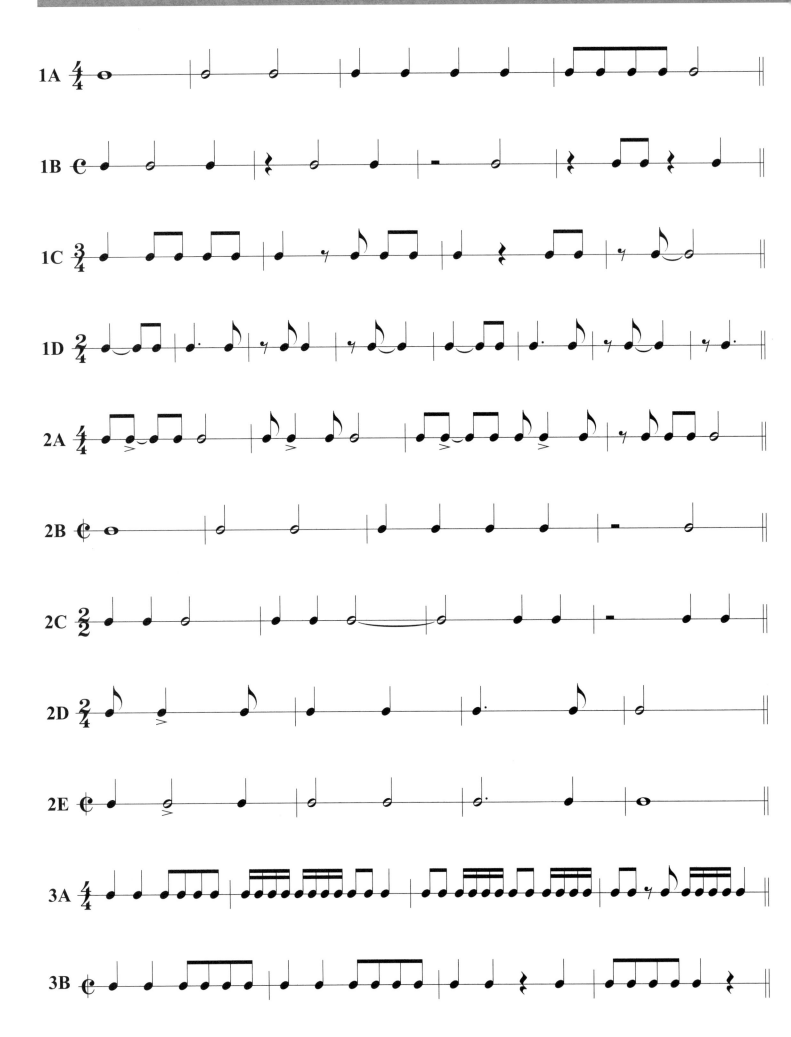

BARITONE VALVE LAYOUT

When reading the fingering chart in this book, valves are presented in this order:

1 2 3
● ● ●

PRACTICING TIPS

Some exercises will be very easy for you to master while others will require more diligent practice. Be prepared to spend more time on the music that is difficult for you. Above all, be consistent in your approach and always end with something fun! The enclosed CDs are a great tool to help you practice, but it is important that you also practice alone.

- Find a **quiet place** where you can practice without distraction.

- Practice at the **same time each day** so it becomes part of your daily schedule.

- Use a **straight back chair** and a **music stand** to promote good posture.

- Begin with a **regular warm-up routine**.

- Practice your **lesson assignments** and **band music**, spending additional time on challenging sections.

- Wrap up your practice by playing **something fun**!

Photograph courtesy of Yamaha Corporation of America

BARITONE FINGERING CHART

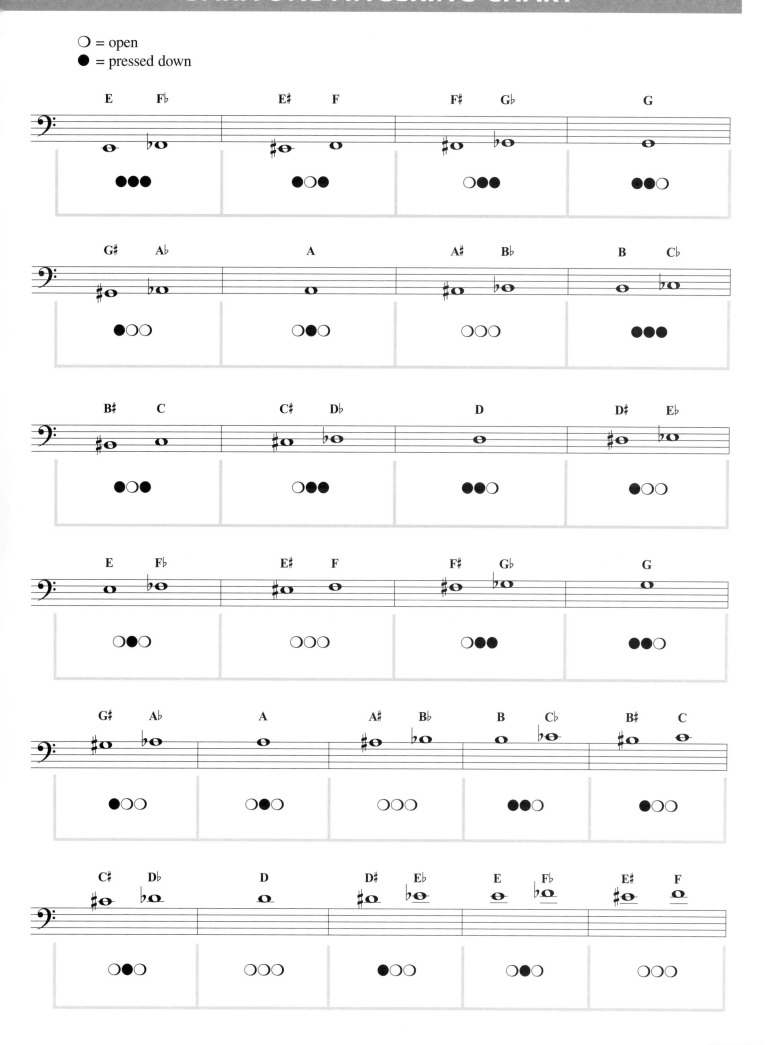

INDEX